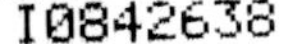

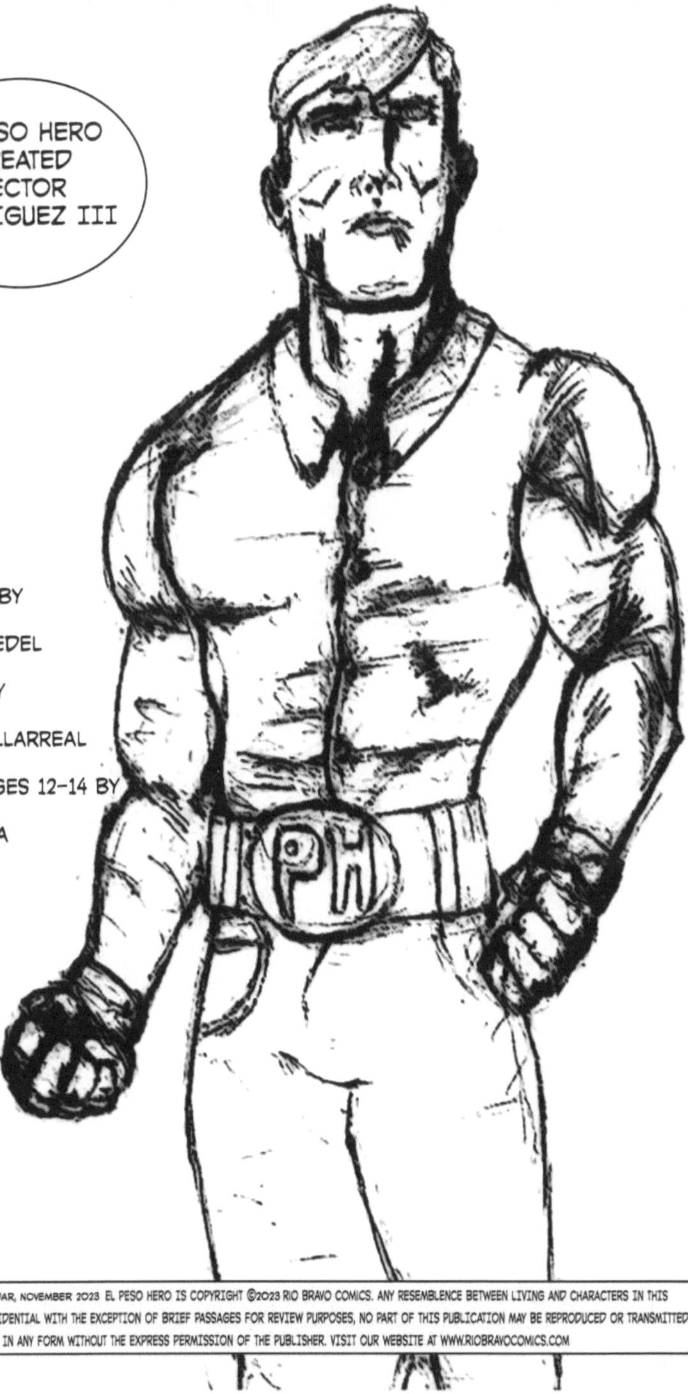

COVER BY

ARIEL MEDEL

ART BY

GUILLERMO VILLARREAL

GUEST ARTIST PAGES 12-14 BY

CHEMA

LOS BRAZOS, COAHUILA MEXICO
EL MODERNO
PURA FIESTA

♪ESTA CANCIÓN QUE CANTO AMIGOS, ES UNA MAS DE DOLOR.♪

♪SI ES QUE ME VEN LLORANDO AMIGOS DISCÚLPENME POR FAVOR.♪
♪Y AHORA TENGO QUE OLVIDARLA TAMBIÉN,Y ARRANCARLA DE MI ALMA Y MI SER.♪
♪Y DE AQUEL AMOR QUE QUEMA MI PIEL, QUE NO QUEDE NADA.♪

♪QUE NO QUEDE HUELLA QUE NO Y QUE NO, QUE NO QUEDE HUELLA.♪
♪PORQUE ESTOY SEGURO QUE TÚ MI AMOR, YA NI ME RECUERDAS.♪

♪QUE NO QUEDE HUELLA QUE NO Y QUE NO, QUE NO QUEDE HUELLA.♪

♪PORQUE ESTOY SEGURO QUE TÚ MI AMOR, YA NI ME RECUERDAS.♪
THE SCRUFFY MAN AT THE BAR HAS BEEN STARING AT YOU.

IT LOOKS LIKE YOU HAVE AN ADMIRER.
MIERDA.

ALGO A SI.
GO SEE WHAT HE WANTS WHILE I FRESHEN UP BEFORE DINNER.

¿QUE QUIERES, COMPA?
GULP
GULP
GULP

CAN I OFFER EL PESO HERO A DRINK?
CAMARERO, AGUA CON LIMON POR FAVOR.
HOW SHOCKING. YOU DON'T DRINK.
¿POR QUÉ ME BUSCAS?
STRAIGHT TO THE POINT.
WHAT I'M ABOUT TO SHARE WITH YOU STAYS CONFIDENTIAL.
I'M COMMANDER ENRIQUE CHONG FROM THE ELITE SPECIAL FORCES TEAM OF COAHUILA.
MY TEAM IS IN A TOUGH SPOT AND WE NEED YOUR HELP, IGNACIO.
ERES DEL GOBIERNO. LO VEO.
NO GRACIAS.
NO QUIERO SER PARTE DE TU CICLO DE VIOLENCIA.

NO SON USTEDES LOS MEJORES DE LOS MEJORES?
RESCATANLO USTEDES.
I KNEW YOU WERE GOING TO SAY SOMETHING LIKE THAT.
TWO MEMBERS OF OUR TEAM HAVE BEEN TAKEN, HOSTAGE.

TANTO QUE GASTAN DINERO EN ARMAS PARA PELIAR LA DELINCUENCIA.
IGNACIO PLEASE LISTEN. THEY WERE CAPTURED BY THE EX-ELEMENTS OF EL CATRIN
YOU HAVE EXPERIENCE WITH THESE PEOPLE.

ARE YOU READY TO GO?
SIEMPRE CON USTEDES HAY ALGO QUE OCULTAN.
THAT WENT BETTER THAN EXPECTED.

VAMOS A CENAR.
QUE TE GUSTARIA COMER? TACOS AL PASTOR?

OUTSKIRTS OF LOS BRAZOS

A VERY FITTING *HUMBLE* HOME IGNACIO.

HE WON'T BE HAPPY WITH YOU FOLLOWING US HERE.
IT'S FOR AN URGENT MATTER FOR THE PEOPLE.
SURE. HE HAS HEARD THAT ONE BEFORE.
TU SABES EL PELIGRO SIGUIENDO ME A CASA?
I'M SORRY IGNACIO, BUT PLEASE JUST LISTEN TO ME. GOOD PEOPLE ARE IN DANGER.

¿QUIERES UN CAFE DE OLLA?
NO, THANK YOU. COFFEE UPSETS MY STOMACH.
I PREFER ZAO CHA.

I'M GOING TO THE SCHOOL.
CALL ME WHEN YOU GET BACK PESO..

MUAH

I HAVE THE SAME SENTIMENT YOU DO WITH OUR GOVERNMENT. THERE IS NO TRUST.

MY FAMILY HAS A COMPLICATED HISTORY IN MEXICO.
WE ARE OF CHINESE DESCENT.

TORREÓN...
15 DE MAYO DE 1911...
DING! DING!
BUEN DÍA SEÑORES, BIENVENIDOS!
VAMOS A NECESITAR ARROZ, FRIJOLES... TODO.
POR SUPUESTO, DISCÚLPEN SEÑORES QUÉ CANTIDAD DE-
Y LO APUNTAS A NUESTRA CUENTA, ...JA JA JA.
JE!
女兒!

CHINO SUCIO.
BANG!

PAPÁ!
MIJA CORRE!
...CORRE A
LA CASA!

VEN PARA ACÁ
ESCUINCLA!
BANG!
BANG!
BANG!
BANG!

BANG!
BANG!

NO!

LETICIA!
LETICIA!

...MIJA!
...MAMÁ, MATARON A PAPÁ! PORQUÉ?! PORQUÉ?!!

...YA LO SÉ.
...VAMOS MIJA, NUESTROS VECINOS NOS ESPERAN, NOS LLEVAN A LA FRONTERA.

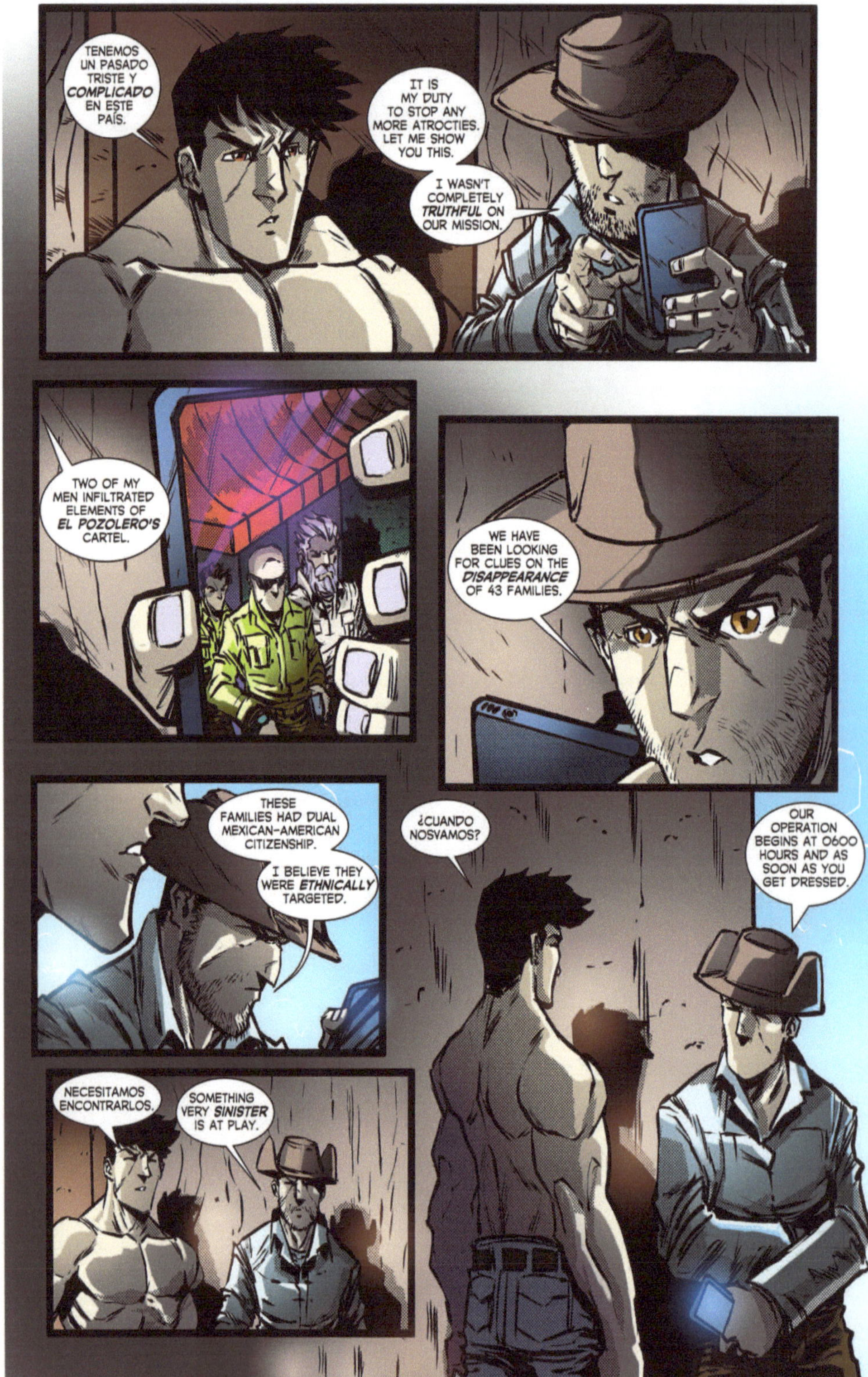

TENEMOS UN PASADO TRISTE Y COMPLICADO EN ESTE PAÍS.
IT IS MY DUTY TO STOP ANY MORE ATROCTIES. LET ME SHOW YOU THIS.
I WASN'T COMPLETELY TRUTHFUL ON OUR MISSION.
TWO OF MY MEN INFILTRATED ELEMENTS OF EL POZOLERO'S CARTEL.
WE HAVE BEEN LOOKING FOR CLUES ON THE DISAPPEARANCE OF 43 FAMILIES.
THESE FAMILIES HAD DUAL MEXICAN-AMERICAN CITIZENSHIP.
I BELIEVE THEY WERE ETHNICALLY TARGETED.
¿CUANDO NOS VAMOS?
OUR OPERATION BEGINS AT 0600 HOURS AND AS SOON AS YOU GET DRESSED.
NECESITAMOS ENCONTRARLOS.
SOMETHING VERY SINISTER IS AT PLAY.

GUERRERO, COAHUILA

THE ELITE 9TH TACTICAL CALVARY BATTALION OF COUIHUILA IS AT THE READY.

ALSO KNOWN AS LA FURIA NEGRA. DEATH RIDES WITH THEM.
ALL JUSTICIEROS NOT LIKE OUR PRESIDENT.
FURIA NEGRA! EL TORO PESADO WILL BE PROVIDING SUPPORT IN OUR MISSION.
YES SIR!
TORO PESADO, YOU RIDE WITH ME.

VILLA UNION, COAHUILA

NOS ESTAN ESPERANDO. EL PUEBLO HA SIDO ABANDONADO.
THE HOSTAGES ARE BEING HELD INSIDE THE LOCAL FUTBOL STADIUM.

HOW THOUGHTFUL OF THEM TO WARN THE CITIZENS. EXPECT A FIGHT IGNACIO.

CHARLIE AND DELTA TAKE THE SOUTH END!
SIR, WE HAVE SPOTTED THE HOSTAGES ON THE FIELD.

ALPHA AND TEAM BRAVO WILL ENGAGE THE HOSTAGES.

WE HAVE CONTACT.
DÉJAME ACERCARME A ELLOS PRIMERO EN CASO DE QUE SEA UNA TRAMPA.
SIR, THE STADIUM IS EMPTY.

SURRENDER NOW OR THIS TOWN WILL BECOME YOUR COFFIN.

WE ARE EVERYWHERE AND SEE EVERYTHING. YOU ARE OUTNUMBERED AND OUTGUNNED.

EL PESO HERO, SHAME ON YOU FOR SIDING WITH THE CORRUPT STATE.
THERE ARE 18 AGENTS VS THOUSANDS OF ROUNDS OF BULLETS. YOU WON'T BE ABLE TO PROTECT THEM ALL.

WHAM
¡¿DONDE ESTAN LAS FAMILIAS?!

IT WASN'T US—

KRUNCH

THEY WEREN'T THE ONES WHO KIDNAPPED THE FAMILIES.
WE UNCOVERED EX-ELEMENTS OF EL CATRIN'S CARTEL REGROUPING. LED BY EL POZOLERO AND A MERC.

SOMEBODY TIPPED THEM OFF THAT WE WERE WORKING UNDERCOVER.
COMMANDANTE, WE HAVE INCOMING.

SKT
WE HAVE A SWARM OF DRONES APPROACHING OUR POSITION. GET READY.
SKT

TEAM BRAVO EXTRACT THE HOSTAGES NOW!

BANG
BANG
BANG
BANG

COMANDANTE! I'VE TRIANGULATED THE SOURCE OF THEIR COMMUNICATIONS.
EL POZOLERO IS THE ONE IN CONTROL OF THE DRONES.

I FORGOT YOU DON'T USE GUNS.
PING
PING
PING

BLAM
BLAM
BLAM
FOOOSH
FOOOSH
FOOOSH
FOOOSH

COVERING FIRE.
RATATATA

ARE YOU OKAY IGNACIO?
SI.

WELL, WHAT DO YOU SAY WE GO GET THESE CABRANOS?
TORO, WE HAVE INTELLIGENCE ON THE LOCATION OF POZOLERO.
¿CUÁL ES TU PLAN?

SIR, MORE DRONES APPROACHING!
PESO HERO, STAY AND DRAW FIRE FROM THE DRONES.
BRAVO TEAM AND I WILL GO AFTER THE SICARIOS.
BOOM
RATATATA

BOOM
RATATATA
RATATATA
SKT ROAD OBSTRUCTIONS AHEAD. PROCEED WITH CAUTION.*SKT*
*SKT*BRAVO, BE READY TO ENCOUNTER HEAVY RESISTANCE.*SKT*

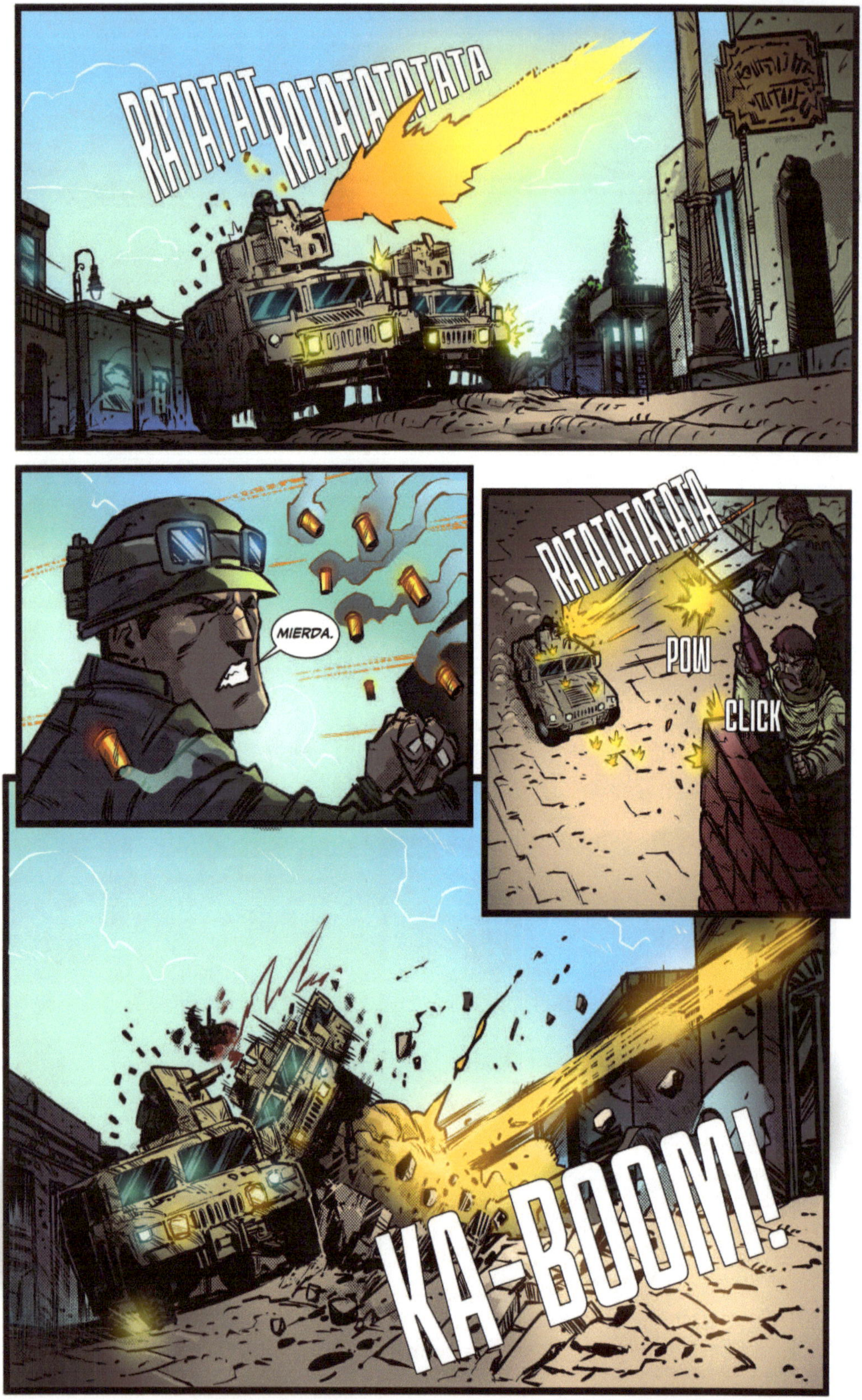

RATATAT RATATATATATA

MIERDA.

RATATATATATA
POW
CLICK

KA-BOOM!

KA-BOOM
VIDEO CLUB
FWD
VHS
CRASH
CHINGADO!
KROOOSH

WHOOSH

KABLAM

BLAM
BLAM
BLAM
CLICK
BLAM

BATOOOM

FZZZZZZZZZZ

THREAT NEUTRALIZE.

CHOK
CHOK
CHOK
CHOK

TANKS AND AMERICAN ATTACK HELICOPTERS--
--WHAT'S GOING ON?!
LLEGUE JUSTO A TIEMPO PARA SALVARTE CON TU SOMBRERO.

COMMANDER CHONG, I'M CAPTAIN ESPINOZA OF THE NEW MEXICAN MECHANIZED ARMY BATTALION OF MONCLOVA.
KOF KOF
WHAT DO YOU THINK OF OUR NEW ISRAELI MARKAVA IV TANKS.
A BIT OVERKILL. WHAT ABOUT OUR FRIENDS ABOVE?
JUST PESKY MILITARY OBSERVERS FROM THE NEW TEXAS GUARD.
vroooom
PESO!
¿NOVA, QUÉ HACES AQUÍ?

NICE TO SEE YOU AGAIN NOVA BUT–
–YOU ARE CURRENTLY IN AN ACTIVE OPERATION. I NEED TO ESCORT YOU OUT.
WE CAME HERE FOR A PERSONAL MATTER.
¿QUE PASA?

I'M WITH LAURA DE LUNA FROM EL DIA BLOG.
SHE CONTACTED ME BECAUSE SHE IS LOOKING FOR IGNACIO. SHE HAS PRESS CLEARANCE.

¿POR QUÉ TE ARRIESGARÍA A TRAERTE AQUÍ?
IN CASE YOU NEEDED CONVINCING.

IGNACIO! THIS IS VERY IMPORTANT WE NEED YOU TO COME WITH US.
PRESS

¿EN SERIO?
HE NEEDS TO TAKE CARE OF PERSONAL BUSINESS.

THANK YOU FOR YOUR HELP IGNACIO.
I KNOW WHERE TO FIND YOU. I'LL LOOK FOR THE MISSING FAMILIES.
SABES DONDE ENCONTRARME.
SÍ SEÑOR.

LA PATRONA'S MANSION.
LAURA, AQUÍ NO HAY NADA PARA MÍ.
I UNDERSTAND IGNACIO BUT THERE IS SOMETHING YOU MUST SEE INSIDE.

¿MI FAMILIA VIVÍA AQUÍ?
YOU LIVED HERE, IGNACIO.
LOOK AT THE PORTRAIT BEHIND YOU.
DO YOU REMEMBER THIS PORTRAIT?
NO, EN ABSOLUTO.
THIS IS THE REASON WE TOOK YOU HERE.

IT'S YOUR FAMILY.

MI PADRES, OLVIDÉ CÓMO SE VEÍAN.
THAT CRYSTAL YOU MADE CONTACT WITH DID MORE THAN GIVE YOU POWERS.

AFECTÓ MI MEMORIA.

MIS ABUELOS...
MIS TÍOS Y MI PRIMO ANGEL...
MI PADRE,
MI QUERIDA MADRE,
MI HERMANA, YO TENÍA UNA HERMANA?!

HER NAME WAS MARICRUZ, SHE WAS WITH YOUR PARENTS WHEN THE AIRPLANE CRASHED.

YOUR SISTER WAS ONLY 10 YEARS OLD.
NECESITO VISITAR SU SEPULCRO.

SHE SURVIDED AND HAS BEEN IN HIDING EVER SINCE.
NOW, ENEMIES OF YOUR FAMILY ARE LOOKING FOR HER IN MEXICO CITY. HER LAST KNOWN LOCATION.

VOY A ENCONTRAR A MI HERMANA EN LA CIUDAD DE MÉXICO.
YOU TWO ARE THE LAST RIVERAS.
WE NEED TO FIND YOUR SISTER BEFORE THEY DO.

UNDISCLOSED LOCATION OFF THE RIO GRANDE
THE STATES OF NUEVO LEON AND TAMAULIPAS WILL NEED EXTRA MEN.
I'LL KEEP THE PRESSURE ON THE STATE POLICE DON'T WORRY.
GOOD. I'LL SECURE THE NORTHERN ROUTES AND REGROUP WHAT'S LEFT OF EL CATRIN'S MEN IN TEXAS.
Coahuila
Nuevo Leon
Tamau

WITH MY BLACKWATER CONNECTIONS AND YOUR RESOURCES. THE BORDER IS OURS.
THAT'S RIGHT, WALKER.
BUZZ BUZZ BUZZ

IT WILL BE BUSINESS AS USUAL. NO MORE FAMILY DRAMA.
CLICK
JEFE!

JEFE, WE HAVE A SITUATION.
JEFE!
WHAT TYPE OF SITUATION!?

SECURITY BREACH.
TERMINATE WITH EXTREME PREJUDICE!
THAT'S IMPOSSIBLE. THIS IS THE MOST SECURE SITE.

SKUTCH

SHOOT IT MEN!
NOBODY OWNS THE BORDER IT HAS NO MASTER. IT ONLY KNOWS FEAR, DEATH AND CHAOS.
MEN?!
A LONG TIME AGO, I WAS BORN AND ABUSED INSIDE AN IMMIGRATION DETENTION FACILITY.
IT WAS A VICIOUS CYCLE.
IT'S TIME FOR A NEW CYCLE OF DEATH AND CHAOS.
WHO GIVES A FU—
EVERYONE ON THE BORDER WILL WELCOME DEATH.
BANG
BANG
BANG
BANG
BANG
BANG
BANG

YO SOY EL CHACAL.
TO BE CONTINUED

EL PESO HERO
RISE OF
MEXICO CITY
COMING SOON